This book belongs to

_____

This book is dedicated to dedicated teacher Becky T. and my board members at Collective for Children.

Copyright © 2025 Grow Grit Press LLC. All rights reserved. No part of this book may be reproduced in any form without permission in writing from the publisher. Please send bulk order requests to info@ninjalifehacks.tv

Paperback ISBN: 979-8-89614-066-5
Hardcover ISBN: 979-8-89614-068-9
eBook ISBN: 979-8-89614-067-2

Printed and bound in the USA.
NinjaLifeHacks.tv

Ninja Life Hacks®
by Mary Nhin

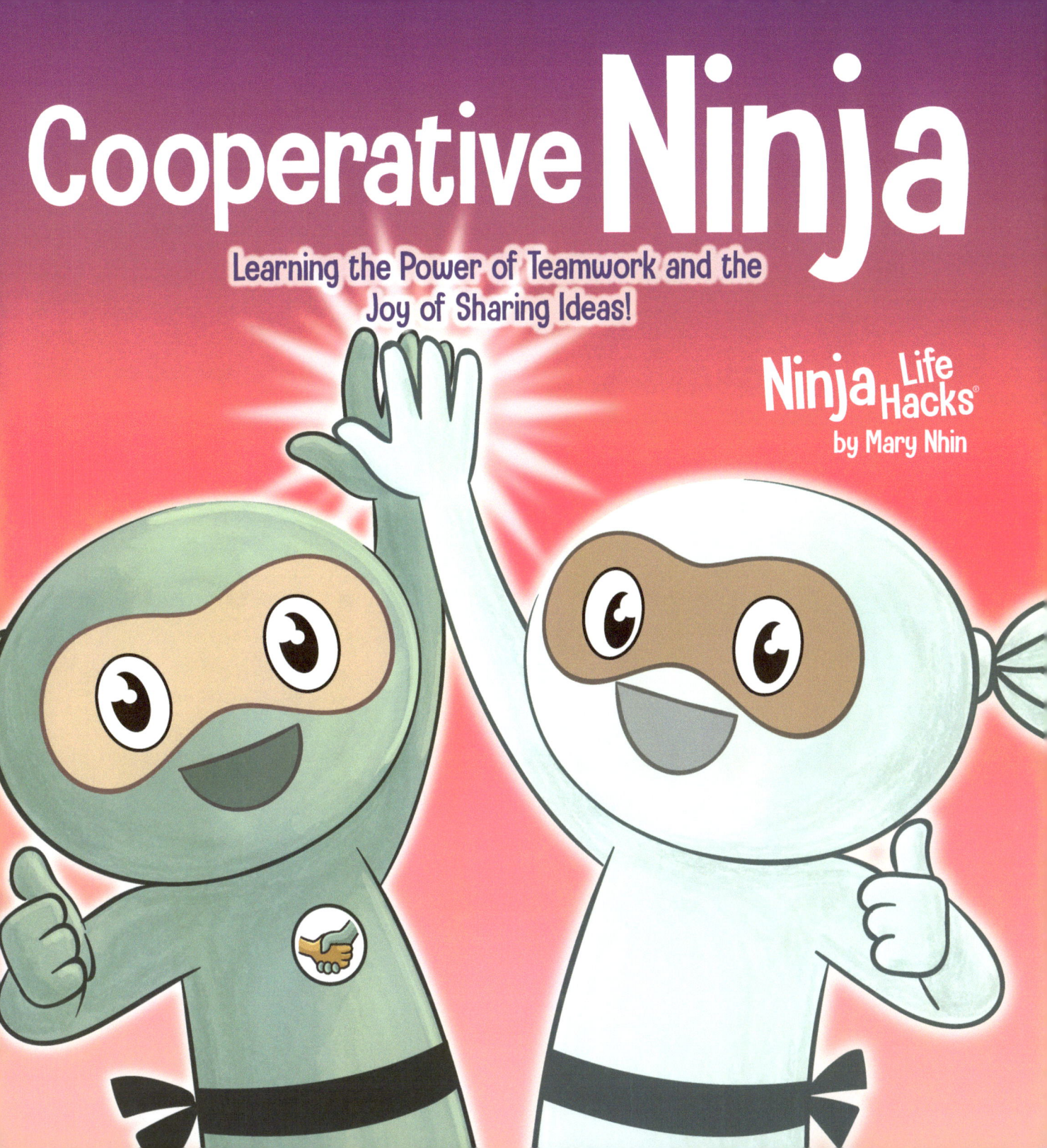

Then one day, Collaborative Ninja taught me a life hack to help me cooperate better with others. It's called the S.H.A.R.E. strategy.

Speak Up – Speak about your ideas and listen to others.
Help Out – Offer help when someone needs it.
Appreciate – Appreciate others by saying something nice.
Respect – Be respectful and take turns.
Engage – Engage others by including them.

Following S.H.A.R.E. makes teamwork better!

Remembering the S.H.A.R.E. strategy can help you be a great team player too!

Check out the fun Cooperative Ninja lesson plans at ninjalifehacks.tv

I love to hear from my readers. Email me your feedback or thoughts on what my next story should be at info@ninjalifehacks.tv   Yours truly, Mary

 @marynhin   @GrowGrit
#NinjaLifeHacks

 Ninja Life Hacks

 Mary Nhin   Ninja Life Hacks

 @officialninjalifehacks